Baby Bunnies

Bobbie Kalman

 Crabtree Publishing Company

www.crabtreebooks.com

It's fun to learn about Baby Animals

Created by Bobbie Kalman

Dedicated by Samantha Crabtree
To two lovely little ladies, Erica and Lola-jane Brown

**Author and
Editor-in-Chief**
Bobbie Kalman

Editor
Kathy Middleton

Proofreader
Crystal Sikkens

Photo research
Bobbie Kalman

Design
Bobbie Kalman
Katherine Berti
Samantha Crabtree (cover)

Production coordinator
Katherine Berti

Special thanks to
Lori Chan and Sarah Chan

Illustrations
Barbara Bedell: page 14 (top)
Bonna Rouse: pages 14 (bottom), 24

Photographs
BigStockPhoto: page 4
Marc Crabtree: pages 1 (background), 11 (bottom left), 24 (pet rabbits)
Dreamstime: pages 9 (top), 20 (bottom), 24 (food chains-ferret
    and habitats)
iStockPhoto: pages 13 (bottom right), 17 (top left), 24 (bodies and
    life cycle-top left)
© Reinhard/ARCO/naturepl.com: page 16
© G. Ronald Austing/Photo Researchers Inc.: page 5
Shutterstock: cover, pages 1 (except background), 3, 6, 7, 8, 9 (bottom),
    10, 11 (except bottom left), 12, 13 (except bottom right), 15,
    17 (except top left), 18, 19, 20 (except bottom), 21, 22, 23,
    24 (except bodies, food chains-ferret, habitats, life cycle-top left,
    and pet rabbits)

Library and Archives Canada Cataloguing in Publication

Kalman, Bobbie, 1947-
    Baby bunnies / Bobbie Kalman.

(It's fun to learn about baby animals)
Includes index.
ISBN 978-0-7787-3958-6 (bound).--ISBN 978-0-7787-3977-7 (pbk.)

    1. Rabbits--Infancy--Juvenile literature. I. Title.
II. Series: It's fun to learn about baby animals

QL737.L32K34 2010   j599.32'139   C2009-905197-4

Library of Congress Cataloging-in-Publication Data

Kalman, Bobbie.
    Baby bunnies / Bobbie Kalman.
        p. cm. -- (It's fun to learn about baby animals)
    Includes index.
    ISBN 978-0-7787-3977-7 (pbk. : alk. paper) -- ISBN 978-0-7787-3958-6
(reinforced library binding : alk. paper)
    1. Rabbits--Juvenile literature. 2. Rabbits--Infancy--Juvenile literature.
I. Title. II. Series.

QL737.L32K35 2010
599.32'139--dc22
                                        2009034831

Crabtree Publishing Company

www.crabtreebooks.com   1-800-387-7650
Printed in China/122009/CT20090915

Published in Canada
Crabtree Publishing
616 Welland Ave.
St. Catharines, Ontario
L2M 5V6

Published in the United States
Crabtree Publishing
350 Fifth Ave.
59th floor
New York, NY 10118

Published in the United Kingdom
Crabtree Publishing
Maritime House
Basin Road North, Hove
BN41 1WR

Published in Australia
Crabtree Publishing
386 Mt. Alexander Rd.
Ascot Vale (Melbourne)
VIC 3032

What is in this book?

Bunny rabbits

A rabbit is an animal called a **mammal**. Mammals have hair or fur on their bodies. Rabbits are covered with fur. Mammals are **born**. They come out of their mothers' bodies. Baby rabbits are called kittens or **bunnies**.

*Bunnies are born in **litters** of three to twelve babies. A litter is more than two babies.*

Mammal mothers feed their babies milk. The milk is made in their bodies. Drinking mother's milk is called **nursing**.

Rabbit relatives

Rabbits are mammals called **lagomorphs**. Rabbits and hares belong to one group of lagomorphs. Pikas belong to another group. Rabbits and hares have large pointed ears. Pikas have short rounded ears.

These baby lagomorphs are rabbits.

Hares have very big ears. They also have long back legs for running and jumping.

Pikas have small rounded ears and short legs.

Wild bunnies

Wild animals live outdoors in natural places called **habitats**. People do not look after them. Some wild rabbits and hares live in **forests**. Forests have many trees. Others live on **mountains**. Mountains are very high places. Some rabbits live in grassy fields called **meadows**. Rabbits and hares also live in dry places called **deserts**.

This hare lives on a mountain.

This black-tailed jackrabbit lives in a desert. Jackrabbits are not really rabbits. They are hares.

This bunny lives in a meadow. There is plenty of food for it to eat.

This rabbit lives in a forest.

Pet bunnies

Some rabbits are **pets**. Pet rabbits live with people. There are many **breeds**, or kinds, of pet rabbits. Rabbits that are the same breed look and act the same. Hares and pikas are wild animals. They are not pets.

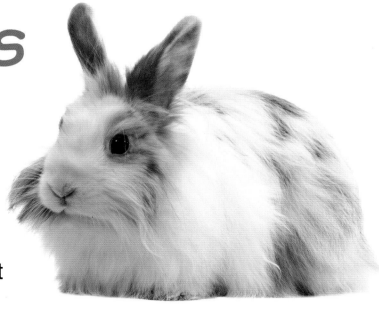

Angora rabbits have long silky fur. They need to be brushed every day.

*This bunny is a **dwarf** bunny. It is smaller than most other rabbits.*

*This black rabbit is a **lop-eared** rabbit. Its ears hang down.*

Some people take their bunnies for walks on leashes.

Bunnies like being with people, too.

Bunnies like being with other bunnies.

Bunny bodies

A bunny has four legs and a tail. Its body is covered with fur. Bunnies have different kinds and colors of fur. Some fur is long and thick, and other fur is short. This rabbit has short fur.

Long ears give rabbits sharp hearing.

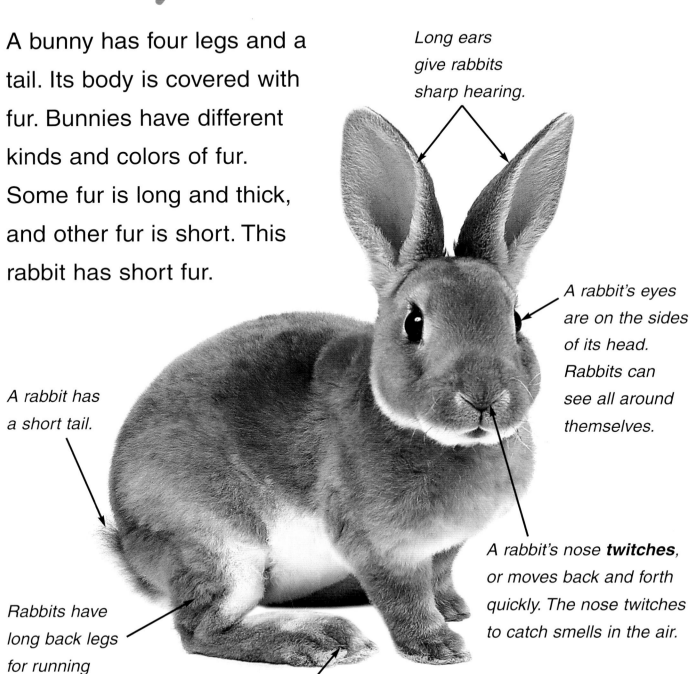

A rabbit's eyes are on the sides of its head. Rabbits can see all around themselves.

A rabbit has a short tail.

A rabbit's nose **twitches**, or moves back and forth quickly. The nose twitches to catch smells in the air.

Rabbits have long back legs for running and hopping.

Rabbits have **claws** on their feet. Claws are curved nails.

These bunnies are all different colors. What colors are they?

A rabbit's front teeth never stop growing.

Bunnies have backbones

Bunnies are **vertebrates**. Vertebrates are animals with **backbones**. Rabbits have strong bodies with many bones inside. All the bones make up a **skeleton**.

rabbit skeleton

backbone

Bunnies have long bones on their back legs. Long legs help bunnies jump.

Bunny burrows

Wild rabbits dig underground homes
in the habitats where they live.
These homes are called **warrens**.
A warren has many **burrows**, or rooms.
The burrows are joined by tunnels.

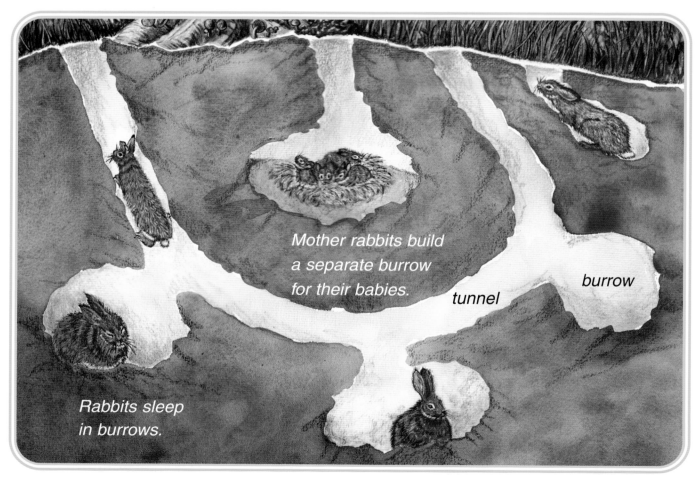

*Mother rabbits build
a separate burrow
for their babies.*

tunnel

burrow

*Rabbits sleep
in burrows.*

These bunnies are peeking out of their warren. Is it safe to come out?

From bunny to rabbit

Bunnies are born blind. They have no fur.

Rabbits have litters of up to 12 bunnies. The bunnies grow and change quickly. They become **adults**. Adults are fully grown rabbits. Adult rabbits can make their own babies.

Baby to adult

Each time a new baby is born, a new **life cycle** begins. A life cycle is the set of changes in an animal from the time it is a baby to the time it becomes an adult.

The life cycle of a rabbit

These pictures show the
life cycle of a rabbit.

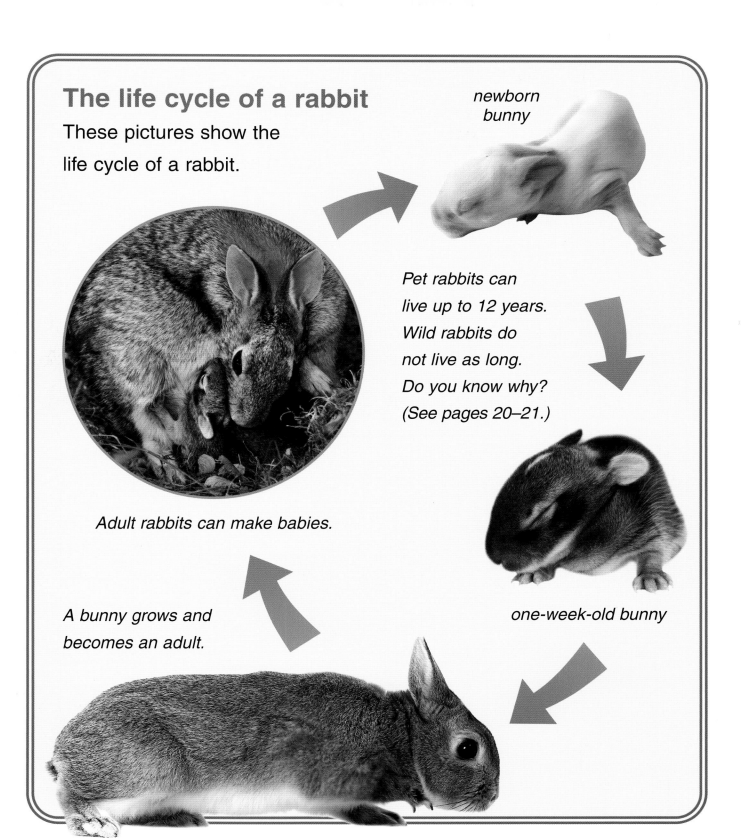

*newborn
bunny*

*Pet rabbits can
live up to 12 years.
Wild rabbits do
not live as long.
Do you know why?
(See pages 20–21.)*

Adult rabbits can make babies.

one-week-old bunny

*A bunny grows and
becomes an adult.*

What do bunnies eat?

Rabbits eat plants. After they are born, bunnies drink their mothers' milk. They nurse for four to five weeks. When they are about two weeks old, they also start eating grass and young plants.

Bunnies eat grass, leaves, bark, and twigs.

Bunnies eat flowers, too.

Pet bunnies eat hay and at least two cups of fresh green vegetables each day.

Lettuce, broccoli, carrots, and celery leaves are good bunny foods. Bunnies also need to drink plenty of fresh, clean water.

What eats bunnies?

Animals eat food to live. Rabbits eat plants. Animals that eat plants are called **herbivores**. **Carnivores** are animals that eat other animals. Foxes, ferrets, wolves, lynxes, hawks, coyotes, and eagles are carnivores. All these carnivores eat rabbits.

Rabbit food

When a carnivore eats a herbivore, there is a **food chain**. The food chain on this page is made up of a plant, a herbivore (rabbit), and a carnivore (ferret). Which other carnivores eat rabbits? See page 21.

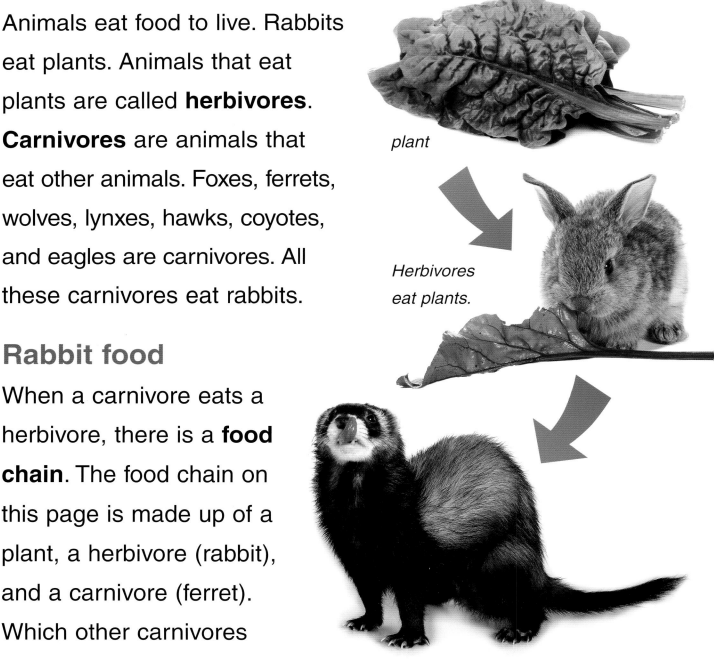

plant

Herbivores eat plants.

Carnivores eat herbivores.

20

Hawks eat rabbits.

Eagles eat rabbits.

Wolves eat rabbits.

Foxes eat rabbits.

Bunny fun

When we think of Easter, we think of bunnies and eggs. Easter is a spring holiday. Bunnies are born in the spring, and eggs **hatch** in spring. To hatch is to come out of an egg. Which of these babies hatches from an egg?

Bunny quiz

There are bunnies, kittens, and chicks in the picture below.

1. Which of the animals are the most like bunnies?

2. Name four ways they are like bunnies.

3. Which of the animals are not like bunnies?

4. Name four ways that they are different.

Words to Know and Index

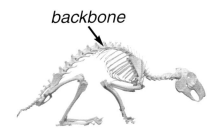
backbone

bodies
pages 4, 5,
12–13

food
pages 9, 18–19,
20–21

food chains
pages 20–21

habitats
pages 8–9, 14

hares
pages 6, 7,
8, 9, 10

life cycle
pages 16–17

pet rabbits
pages 10–11,
17, 19

pikas
pages 6, 7, 10

warrens
pages 14–15

wild rabbits
pages 8–9,
10, 14, 17

24